HOW IT WORKS

TELEPHONE AND THE INTERNET

James Nixon

W

First published in 2009 by
Franklin Watts
338 Euston Road
London NW1 3BH

Franklin Watts Australia
Level 17/207 Kent Street
Sydney NSW 2000

Copyright © 2009 Franklin Watts

ISBN: 978 0 7496 8409 9

Dewey classification number: 384

A CIP catalogue record for this book is available
from the British Library.

Planning and production by Discovery Books Limited
Editor: James Nixon
Designer: Ian Winton
Illustrations: Stefan Chabluk
Commissioned photography: Bobby Humphrey

Photographs: Alamy Images: p. 14 top (Brinkstock); Getty Images: pp. 8 (Bell
Collection/National Geographic), 14 bottom (Hoby Finn), 15 (Harrison/Topical Press Agency),
18 top (Darren Robb); Istockphoto.com: pp. 19 (Christopher Jones), 22 bottom (Matjaz
Boncina), 24, 25 top (Yvonne Chamberlain); Newscast: pp. 16 (Gabriel Szabo), 26 (David
Parry); Shutterstock: pp. 6 bottom (J. Gatherum), 7 top, bottom (Monkey Business Images),
9 top (Jeff Thrower), 9 middle (Margo Harrison), 9 bottom, 10 (Lim Yong Hian), 12, 16 top
(David Hughes), 17 top (Jerry Horbert), 17 bottom (Beto Gomez), 18 top (Norman Pogson),
21 top, 21 middle (Andrew Barker), 21 bottom, 22 top, 23 middle (Stuart Monk), 23 bottom,
25 middle (Petar Tasevski).

Cover photos: Bobby Humphrey: bottom; Istockphoto.com: title background (Andrey Volodin),
bottom right (Matjaz Boncina); Shutterstock: top.

Printed in China

Franklin Watts is a division of Hachette Children's Books,
an Hachette UK company.
www.hachette.co.uk

Contents

Words in bold are in the glossary on page 28.

It's good to talk

Everybody likes to chat with their friends. But how do you speak to a friend or relative who lives in a different village or town? What if they live on the other side of the world?

To **communicate** with each other over long distances we use machines such as telephones, mobile phones and computers.

Life without phones

Hundreds of years ago sharing information with people who lived far away was very difficult. Imagine what life was like before the telephone was invented. How did people make plans or keep in touch with each other? You could send a letter, but this was very slow.

Small world

Over time machines were invented to make communication faster and easier. Nowadays your voice can be directly heard by someone living in a different country. On the Internet messages can be sent almost immediately.

Whenever you are using a phone or the Internet there is an amazing amount of **technology** working to make contact with your friend possible. This book will tell you how this technology works.

The first telephones

The first successful telephone was designed by Alexander Graham Bell in 1876. 'Tele' and 'phone' are the Greek words that mean 'talking from a distance'.

Amazing discovery

Bell (right) knew that your voice could be turned into an electrical signal and sent down a long piece of wire. At the other end the signal could be turned back into the sound of your voice. The telephone has since become one of the most common household **appliances** in the world.

Early phones

The first telephones were quite large and had no **dial** or keypad. The caller picked up the receiver and gave a phone number to an **operator**. When the phone rang it was not an electronic bleeper like it is today – it was a real bell ringing on the phone.

Bell

Receiver

Mouthpiece

Later on phones had a dial for entering a phone number (left). Nowadays we use a simple keypad.

Cordless phones

Today, we can walk around the house while talking on the phone. Cordless phones can be taken off their base but stay connected using radio signals.

Inside a phone

Your telephone is connected by a line to a phone socket in the wall. It can send and receive sound.

Look at this ordinary handset. There is a **loudspeaker** at the top which you hold to your ear to hear sound. At the bottom is a **microphone** that you hold to your mouth and speak into to send sound.

Loudspeaker

In and out

Coming out of your handset is a coil of cable. If it is a cordless phone the cable comes out of the base. Inside are two pairs of copper wires which carry sound as electrical signals. One pair carries your voice as a signal away from the microphone. The other pair carries your friend's voice as a signal to the loudspeaker.

Microphone

Sound as signals

So how is the sound of your voice changed into an electrical signal? A simple microphone contains a thin piece of plastic (diaphragm) attached to a metal coil. When you speak into the microphone the plastic **vibrates** and moves the coil towards an **electromagnet**.

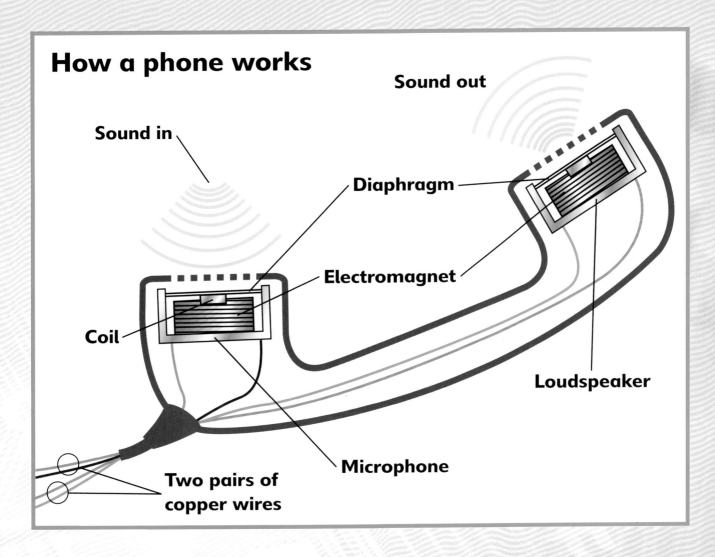

How a phone works

Sound out

Sound in

Diaphragm

Electromagnet

Coil

Loudspeaker

Microphone

Two pairs of copper wires

This **magnetism** turns the sound energy in your voice into **electrical energy**. The loudspeaker works in almost the same way. It is just wired in the opposite direction.

Making a call

The first thing you do when you make a telephone call is pick up the handset. Picking up the handset is like flicking a switch. It turns on a **circuit** of electricity that runs between your phone and the telephone **network** (see page 16).

Dialling

Next you dial the number of your friend. We still say dial even though most phones now have buttons that you press.

Phone numbers

Most home telephone numbers in the UK are 11 digits long and have two parts. The first few numbers are the 'area code'. The most usual form is a five-digit area code followed by another six digits. For example, the area code for Dundee is 01382 and Hull is 01482. Some big towns have a slightly different system. London numbers start with 020 followed by nine digits.

Tones

If you listen down the phone before you dial you should hear the 'dialling tone'. This shows you that the network is ready for your call. There are other tones, too. You will hear a ringing tone while you wait for the person to answer. An 'engaged tone' tells you that the line is busy.

Phone codes for some UK towns and cities

Aberdeen 01224
Dundee 01382
Edinburgh 0131
Glasgow 0141
Belfast 02890
Tyne and Wear and Durham 0191
Leeds 0113
Hull 01482
Liverpool 0151
Manchester 0161
Sheffield 0114
Nottingham 0115
Leicester 0116
Norwich 01603
Birmingham 0121
Aberystwyth 01970
Cardiff 029
Bristol 0117
London 020
Southampton and Portsmouth 023
Exeter 01392

At the exchange

How does pressing a series of numbers connect you to the right person?

A building called a telephone exchange (right) in your local area receives your call and routes it on to the person you want to speak to.

Connecting you up

When you dial a number on your telephone, listen to the musical notes it sends down the line. The exchange knows which person you are calling by the musical sounds your handset makes and connects your telephone lines together.

If you are phoning someone nearby, your local exchange will connect your call. The local exchange is connected to all the telephone lines in your area.

Telephone exchange

For long distance calls the call has to be routed through a series of exchanges until it reaches the exchange nearest to the person you have dialled.

Switchboards

In the past connecting calls at the exchange was done by an operator. They would take your phone line, and connect it by hand to another phone line by plugging it into a socket on a wooden board. This was called a switchboard.

Nowadays computers have replaced switchboards. They work in the same way, but they connect people's telephone lines automatically. All this happens in seconds.

Carrying calls

The telephone network is a vast system of wires. Nearly every home has a telephone line, which is connected to a local exchange, and from there to a main exchange in a large city.

Most calls go from homes to exchanges along copper wires. They are usually carried by **telegraph poles** high above the ground (right). Modern lines may run underground.

The telephone line leaves your home and usually leads to a green cabinet in your street (left). This contains the telephone lines for a group of houses. A cable from the box then carries the lines away to the exchange and the main telephone network.

Glass wires

Some phone lines no longer use the old copper wires. Your voice can now be carried down fibre optic cables. Optical fibres are strands of very pure glass that are as thin as a human hair. Thousands of these fibres are packed together in bundles in a fibre optic cable. One cable can carry thousands of telephone calls at the same time, so fewer cables need laying.

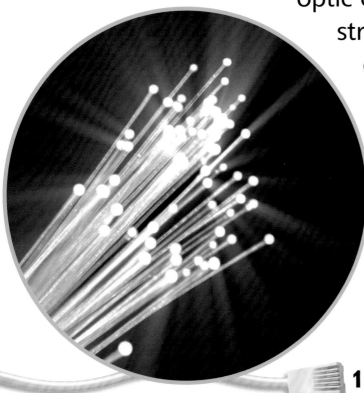

Mobile phones

The home is not the only place you can make a telephone call. Mobile phones now let you make calls from nearly anywhere.

You can be at the beach, on a train, or on top of a mountain – it doesn't matter. Mobiles do not use wires.

Keep in touch

Twenty years ago few people had a mobile phone. If you broke down in your car and needed help you had to find a public telephone box. Now we can keep in contact with each other wherever we go.

Through the air

When you speak into a mobile phone your voice is changed into electrical signals and then packed into radio waves. The radio signal is zapped through the air at the **speed of light** until it reaches the nearest mobile phone mast (left).

Antennas

Masts have huge, high **antennas** that pick up the signals and route them across the country. The radio signal is passed through an exchange to another mast near to the phone you are calling. The signal is then sent on to the phone itself. Sometimes a phone cannot receive a signal if it is too far from a mast.

Around the world

In the past making a long-distance call could take a while. Today your phone calls abroad are made in the blink of an eye.

New telephone lines using fibre optic cables send your voice as a beam of light instead of as an electrical signal. This allows your calls to travel super fast.

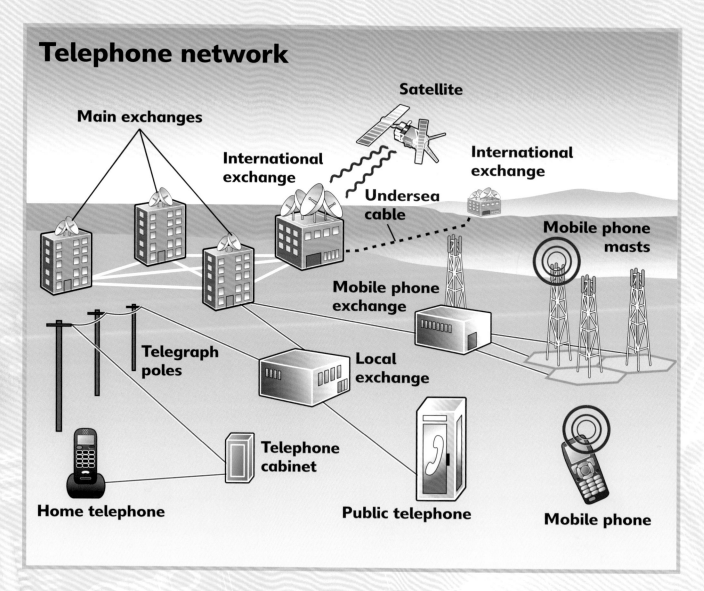

Telephone network

Satellite

Main exchanges

International exchange

International exchange

Undersea cable

Mobile phone masts

Mobile phone exchange

Telegraph poles

Local exchange

Telephone cabinet

Home telephone

Public telephone

Mobile phone

Long-distance calls can also be bounced across the world as a radio signal using **microwave** towers (bottom) or even **satellites** in space (left).

▲ Huge dishes are used to send and receive signals via satellites.

▲ **Microwave tower**

Under the sea
Nearly all the exchanges in the world are connected to each other. If you are phoning someone in the USA, your call goes on a long journey through a cable that runs all the way under the Atlantic Ocean. The cable is called the 'transatlantic telephone' or TAT for short. Since 1988 TAT has used fibre optics.

The Internet

The Internet connects millions and millions of computers across the world.

You have probably used it yourself. It is a place to shop, share information and chat with your friends. But did you know it works by using the same phone lines and satellite signals that you use to make your telephone calls?

Logging on

To get on the Internet your computer plugs into the phone socket in your wall, just like your ordinary telephone. Computer information is changed into a form that can be carried on telephone lines.

Broadband

Many people have a broadband (ADSL) Internet service. Computers on broadband send signals down the telephone line that do not block voice signals, so you can use the Internet and your telephone at the same time. A tiny box called a microfilter (right) separates the different signals coming into your home.

ADSL Filter

Wi-Fi adaptor

Wireless

Wi-Fi

Even a laptop computer without wires can use the Internet. If you are in a **Wi-Fi** area and have a Wi-Fi adaptor, Internet data can be sent between computers using radio signals.

Internet services

There are many ways to communicate with each other using the Internet.

E-mail

You can send messages from one computer to another. This is known as e-mail. Internet users have an e-mail address just like they have a house address. Unlike a letter you put in the post, an e-mail can arrive in seconds.

Chatting

You can make and receive telephone calls on the Internet using microphones and loudspeakers built into the computer. Or you can just plug a handset into the back of it.

However, the Internet can go a step further than a telephone.

Using a webcam (below) you can also send live pictures of yourself to the person you are talking to.

Webcam

The Web

Using the Internet to search the World Wide Web is very popular. On the Web are millions of pages of information and entertainment that have been created by different computers all over the world.

Shopping online

You can now do the shopping without leaving the house. Many companies use the Web to sell their services and products. Payment can be made over the Internet, too.

Charging you

Although there is one network of wires and just one phone line coming into your home, there are a number of companies who can provide you with communication services.

You can choose to have your Internet, phone and mobile calls all supplied by different companies.

Bills

The company tracks how much you use your phone or Internet and sends you a bill.

Look at these bills. Each call you make is timed and recorded by the phone company so they know exactly how much to charge you. On top of your call costs there is a set charge for having a telephone line connected to your home.

How much?

The cost of a phone call depends on where the person you are calling lives. If they live far away your call could be more expensive.

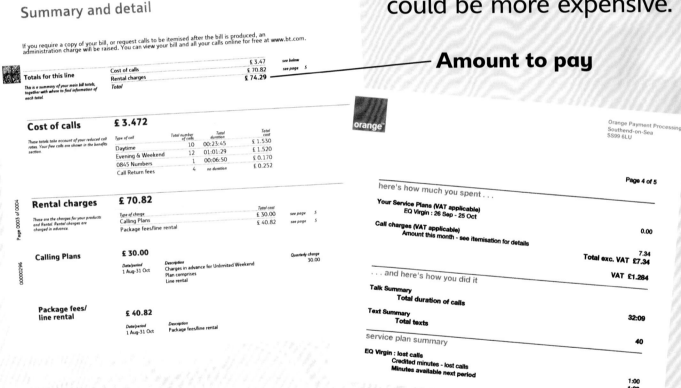

Amount to pay

Using your phone and Internet in the evening is often cheaper than in the day.

It all depends on the service you have bought from the company. Some people pay a fixed amount each month. This lets you use your phone lines as much as you want.

Glossary

Antennas Rods, wires or other structures that receive and send radio signals.

Appliances Machines designed to carry out a particular job.

Circuit A complete path which an electrical current can flow around.

Communicate Share or exchange information.

Dial A disc on a telephone with numbered finger holes. The disc is turned for each number dialled in a telephone number.

Electrical energy Energy that comes from electricity.

Electromagnet A magnet which works by electricity.

Loudspeaker A piece of equipment that turns electrical signals into sound.

Magnetism A force between two metal objects, such as attraction or repulsion.

Microphone An instrument used for turning sound waves into electrical energy which can then be transmitted.

Microwave An electromagnetic wave with shorter wavelength than normal radio waves. Microwaves are used in communications.

Network A large system of electrical lines, pipes or roads, which connect at many points.

Operator A person who works at the switchboard of a telephone exchange.

Radio signals Electrical waves sent through the air. They are used by mobile and cordless phones to carry sound messages.

Satellites Machines sent into orbit around the Earth. They can send and receive telephone signals.

Speed of light Nothing is quicker than the speed of light. It travels at about 300,000 kilometres per second (186,000 miles per second).

Technology The use of science to do practical things.

Telegraph poles Tall poles used to carry telephone wires above the ground.

Vibrates Shakes rapidly.

Wi-Fi In Wi-Fi areas, users access the Internet via a central hub, which is connected to a phone line.

Further information

Books

Bell and the Science of the Telephone, Brian Williams, 2005 (Book House)

My First Internet Guide, Chris Oxlade, 2007 (Heinemann)

Telecommunications (Technology All Around Us), Anne Rooney, 2005 (Franklin Watts)

Websites

www.explainthatstuff.com/cellphones.html
This is an introduction to mobile phones and how they work.

www.howstuffworks.com
On this website you can find out about the technology behind many things including long-distance calls, cordless phones and fibre optics.

www.connected-earth.com/LearningCentre/index.htm
Here you can find how telecommunications work via a range of interactive activities.

Note to parents and teachers: Every effort has been made by the Publishers to ensure that these websites are suitable for children, that they are of the highest educational value, and that they contain no inappropriate or offensive material. However, because of the nature of the Internet, it is impossible to guarantee that the contents of these sites will not be altered. We strongly advise that Internet access is supervised by a responsible adult.

Index